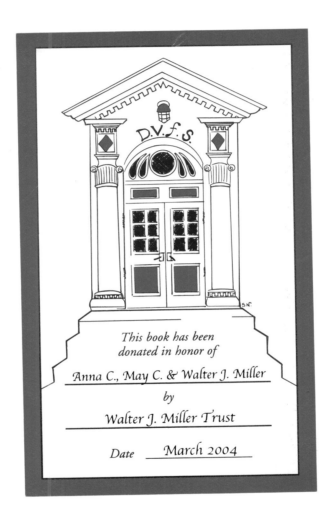

D.V.F.S.

This book has been
donated in honor of

Anna C., May C. & Walter J. Miller

by

Walter J. Miller Trust

Date   March 2004

Life and Death in Hitler's Europe

Jane Shuter

Heinemann Library
Chicago, Illinois

Designed by Joanna Sapwell and Tinstar Design
Illustrations by Martin Griffin
Originated by Ambassador Litho Ltd
Printed in China, by Wing King Tong

07 06 05 04 03
10 9 8 7 6 5 4 3 2 1

**Library of Congress
Cataloging-in-Publication Data**
Shuter, Jane.
  Life and death in Hitler's Europe / Jane Shuter.
    p. cm. -- (The Holocaust)
Summary: An account of what life was like in Europe for both Jews and non-Jews while Adolf Hitler was in power.
Includes bibliographical references and index.
  ISBN 1-4034-0811-4 (HC) 1-4034-3203-1 (Pbk.)
  1. Holocaust, Jewish (1939–1945) – Europe – Juvenile literature. 2. National socialism–Europe–Juvenile literature. 3. Hitler, Adolf, 1889–1945–Juvenile literature. 4. Jews–Persecutions–Europe–Juvenile literature. [1. Holocaust, Jewish (1939–1945) 2. National socialism. 3. Hitler, Adolf, 1889–1945. 4. Jews–Persecutions–Europe.] I. Title. II. Series: Holocaust
(Chicago, Ill.)
  DS135.E83 S62 2003
  940.53'18--dc21
                                    2002006847

Acknowledgments
The author and publisher are grateful to the following for permission to reproduce copyright material: p. 4 Ulstein Bilderdienst; pp. 6, 14 Topham Picturepoint; pp. 7, 15, 18, 25, 41, 46 AKG; pp. 8, 28, 32, 33 Mary Evans Picture Library; pp. 9, 10, 21, 31 BPK; pp. 11, 19 Bilderdienst Suddeutscher Verlag; pp. 12, 26 (top), 26 (bottom) Tomi Ungerer & Digenes Verlag/AG Zurich; pp. 13, 34, 35, 39, 44 Yad Vashem; p. 17 Wiener Forman; p. 20 Tomi Ungerer Collection; pp. 22, 24, 48 Robert Hunt Library; p. 23 Popperfoto; pp. 27 Unknown; p. 29 Roger Scruton/De Campo Films; pp. 30, 37, 40, 46, 47, 49 USHMM; p. 38 Jewish Museum, Frankfurt; p. 45 Paul Soros

Cover photograph reproduced with the permission of Mary Evans Picture Library.

Special thanks to Ronald Smelser and Sally Brown-Winter.

About the series consultants
Ronald Smelser is a history professor at the University of Utah. He has written or edited eight books on the Holocaust and Nazi Germany and over three dozen articles. His recent publications include *Learning About the Holocaust: A Student Guide* (4 vol.) and *Lessons and Legacies: The Holocaust and Justice*. Professor Smelser is also a past president of the German Studies Association.

Sally Brown-Winter has worked in the field of Jewish Education as a principal and teacher for over 25 years. In her schools, the Shoah—its history, lessons, and implications—have been explored from kindergarten through high school.

Every effort has been made to contact copyright holders of any material reproduced in this book. Any omissions will be rectified in subsequent printings if notice is given to the publisher.

Some words are shown in bold, **like this.** You can find out what they mean by looking in the glossary.

Contents

The Occupation of Europe

In 1933 the **Nazi** Party, led by Adolf Hitler, came to power and became the only political party in Germany. The Nazis wanted to create a huge German empire called the **Third Reich.** Between 1938 and 1945, the German army marched into and **occupied** much of Europe, including Poland, France, the Netherlands, and parts of the Soviet Union, nearly defeating the forces of the British Empire, France, and the U.S.S.R. During this period, the Nazis systematically killed off many people they thought of as "**undesirable.**" The largest group of people killed were the **Jewish** people. The Nazis killed between five and six million Jews in what has become known as the **Holocaust.** They were trying to destroy all of the Jewish people in the areas they controlled.

Why Did the German Army Invade?

Once in power, the Nazis banned all other political parties and began trying to create the perfect Nazi state. One thing the Nazis wanted was *Lebensraum*—more land for Germans to live in. To begin, the Nazis took land that had once been part of Germany. Once the German army was on the march, though, it continued, north, south, east, and west of Germany. One of Hitler's beliefs was that a strong country had the right to take over a weaker one.

The German Army

When Germany lost **World War I** in 1918, the **Treaty of Versailles** took a lot of land from Germany and reduced the size of its army and navy. When the Nazis took over in 1933, Hitler began to build the army up again, breaking the Treaty of Versailles. This photo shows the German army marching into the Rhineland in 1936. The terms of the Treaty banned the army from this part of Germany, which shared a border with France. Hitler admitted to his generals: "The 45 hours after the march into the Rhineland were the most nerve-wracking of my life." His army was still small and he feared that the other European countries would stop it. If they had known what Hitler planned, they might have done so. However, at this point, they were still trying to prevent war.

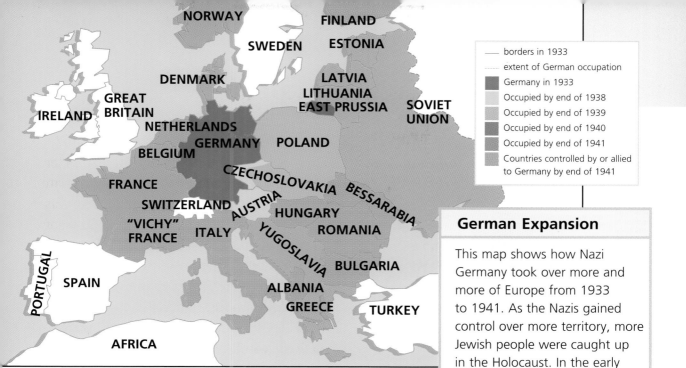

This map shows how Nazi Germany took over more and more of Europe from 1933 to 1941. As the Nazis gained control over more territory, more Jewish people were caught up in the Holocaust. In the early 1930s, many Jews left Germany for the safety of France, the Netherlands, or Belgium, only to find these countries taken over by Germany during the war.

Map legend:
- borders in 1933
- extent of German occupation
- Germany in 1933
- Occupied by end of 1938
- Occupied by end of 1939
- Occupied by end of 1940
- Occupied by end of 1941
- Countries controlled by or allied to Germany by end of 1941

Why Did No One Stop the Nazis?

Other European countries did not try to stop the Nazis for several reasons. One reason was that they did not want another war like World War I. Another was that Hitler did not say: "I want to take over as much of Europe as possible." Instead, he claimed he was putting right the injustice of the Treaty of Versailles. Many Europeans agreed that the treaty had been too harsh. Hitler began by moving his army into the Rhineland. Then, in 1938, he took over Austria, where more than 80 percent of the population was German. The other major European powers, France, Italy, and Britain, then agreed Hitler could make one "last territorial claim in Europe" and take over the **Sudetenland,** a part of Czechoslovakia, with a large German-speaking population. However, in March 1939, he took over the rest of Czechoslovakia, and in September 1939, he invaded Poland. At this point, Britain and France, who had promised to help Poland if it was invaded, declared war.

They were too late. While they had been concentrating on peace, Hitler had been preparing for war. In a speech made in 1940, Joseph Goebbels, Hitler's **propaganda** minister, announced: "When the war is over we want to be masters of Europe."

How Do We Know?

We know about life in Nazi-occupied Europe from many different sources. People made written accounts, diaries, poems, and pictures. A lot of Nazi propaganda still exists that shows how the Nazis took control of all aspects of life. Lastly, many TV programs and movies have been made about the war. These programs and movies include interviews with all kinds of people who lived in Hitler's Europe.

The Nazis Take Over

Before the **Nazis** came to power in 1933, Germany was a **democracy,** like most of the rest of Europe. It was also suffering an economic depression, or a time of high unemployment, low wages, and high prices. The German government had not been able to solve the country's economic problems. The Nazis claimed democracy was not working and promised to make Germany great again. They said Germany needed one political party and one leader—and that leader was Adolf Hitler.

Enough voters in Germany agreed with the Nazis that they were able to get the most seats in the *Reichstag*, the German parliament. Once they controlled the *Reichstag*, the Nazis engineered Hitler's appointment as Chancellor, then they took over completely by banning all other political parties. They began to turn Germany into the "perfect" Nazi state. The Nazis' next priority was to expand their **Lebensraum,** which meant finding more "living space" for the Germans. Their solution was to invade and take over other countries.

Blitzkrieg

Instead of sending in long lines of slow-marching soldiers, the Nazis used a new tactic called **blitzkrieg,** or "lightning war." First, they sent their planes to bomb the enemy's air force, roads, railways, and telephone lines. Then they sent in fast-moving troops. Blitzkrieg was led by tanks, the Panzer division, and light artillery. These troops were protected by the German air force, which also bombed enemy troops. Most other European armies could not cope with the speed and ferocity of the German advance and were defeated in a matter of weeks.

"Undesirables"

To the Nazis, all countries, even Germany, had people who were "**undesirable.**" People were undesirable because of their race, religion, opposition to the Nazis, or even their health. **Jewish** people, **gypsies,** homosexuals, the physically and mentally disabled, and **Jehovah's Witnesses** were all considered to be undesirable. Undesirables had to change their ways when possible to fit the Nazi pattern or leave Nazi-**occupied** lands. If they did neither, they had to be cut off from "ordinary **citizens,**" or even be killed. The gypsies in this photo are being rounded up and taken to **concentration camps.**

Influence

The Germans controlled some countries by influence. In other words, if another country agreed with Nazi views, they were seen as allies and allowed to keep their own government. At the start of the war, Italy, which was ruled by the fascist dictator Benito Mussolini, was one such country. The Nazis also made agreements with the leaders of countries that were not sympathetic to Nazi views. These leaders could still run their countries—as long as they did so the way the Nazis told them to. However, if an allied country did not completely support Nazi policies, it soon became an enemy of Germany—this reversal happened to both Italy and the Soviet Union. The German army marched in and influence quickly became occupation.

A Different View

The Nazis had strong ideas about **racial superiority.** They treated the people in the countries they took over in different ways, depending on how they fit into Nazi ideas about **race.** German soldiers were taught that people such as the Slavs, who included the Poles and the Russians, were inferior races. One soldier advancing into Poland said:

> I do not understand how these people are biologically capable of staying alive. Also they live in indescribably filthy conditions. The Polish Jews have alien-looking faces.

On the other hand, German soldiers were taught that "**Aryans**" were the best race. Although the people of Scandinavia, Britain, and France were not as important as the Germans, they were not thought to be *untermenschen*, or "subhuman," like the Slavs. So the German army, Nazi officials, and police behaved far better toward the people of France than they did to the people of Poland—as long as they did as they were told.

The Nazis and the Holocaust

Of all the groups of people that Adolf Hitler despised as "inferiors," he hated **Jewish** people the most. This hatred was clear even before the **Nazis** came to power in Germany. Once they were in power, they began to act against Jews immediately.

Step by Step

The Nazis began by passing laws that stopped Jews from working in certain jobs. They moved on to pass laws that stopped Jews from using the same transportation, schools, public facilities, even park benches as non-Jews. Then they began working to make Germany and the countries it controlled **Judenfrei**—Jew free. In occupied countries, Jews were herded into walled-off **ghettos** in cities and were not allowed to live anywhere else. Once Jews were cut off from other people, it was easier for the Nazis to work even further against them.

The Holocaust

The Nazis had tried to force the Jews in Germany to leave the country before the war. After war broke out, German policy against the Jews became more and more severe. Eventually, they moved on to what they called the "Final Solution." They set up **death camps** at Chelmno, Belzec, Sobibor, Treblinka, Majdanek, and Auschwitz-Birkenau. The only purpose of these camps was to kill Jewish people.

Mein Kampf

In 1923, Hitler and the Nazis had tried to take power in Germany by force. They failed, and Hitler was sent to prison. While he was in prison, the Nazi Party fell apart. During the eight months Hitler spent in prison, he wrote a book called *Mein Kampf* or "My Struggle", outlining his beliefs. Once the Nazis came to power in 1933, everyone was expected to read this book. In it, Hitler clearly says that he thought Jewish people were ruining Germany and that they must not be allowed to be German **citizens.**

Targets of Hatred

Once they were in power, the Nazis lost no time in persecuting Jews. They started by trying to get people not to buy goods from Jews. These Nazis are going around urging German people not to shop at Jewish stores. In many cases, the Nazis stood guard over the stores hoping to frighten people away.

Visible Camps

Some camps, like death camps, were hidden from view. Many camps, though, such as Plaszów shown here, were close enough to towns for the townspeople to have known about the camp and to have seen the prisoners.

Who Knew?

No one in Nazi-controlled countries could have been in any doubt that the Nazis hated and persecuted Jewish people. However, people disagree over how much ordinary people knew about what went on in the camps and during the **Holocaust.** Immediately after the war, historians often suggested that most people knew nothing about the Holocaust and that the Nazis kept their activities secret. Some later historians have suggested the exact opposite—that almost everyone knew. It is more likely that different people knew different things, depending on where they lived. A farming family living well away from any camps or cities, who only read Nazi-approved newspapers and listened to Nazi-run radio, was much less likely to know the truth about the camps than a family that lived near a camp.

Who Agreed?

Not everyone in Nazi Germany accepted Nazi beliefs, even if they had to seem to agree in order to stay out of the camps. Some of them even worked secretly against the Nazis. On the other hand there were a lot of people, especially in Germany itself, who were almost hypnotized by the Nazis, and who accepted all Nazi **propaganda** as truth. There were also political groups in other countries that shared Nazi beliefs, including their beliefs about **race.** These groups were happy to **collaborate** with the Nazis.

Different Parts of the Reich

The **Nazis** thought of the land they had taken over in different ways. Some places, such as Alsace, which had been made a part of France after **World War I**, were thought of as "regained" parts of Germany. They were governed as part of Germany.

Other places, such as parts of pre-war Poland, were to become part of a "Greater Germany" in time. They were run by German officials. The **Gestapo** and **SS** were sent in to keep order. The army itself moved out, unless there was fighting on the borders, (as in the fighting between Germany and Russia in Poland in 1942–4).

Finally, there were countries like France and Greece. Neither had ever been part of Germany and both had long histories as separate countries. These countries had to be controlled by the army as well as German officials, the Gestapo, and the SS.

Nazi Ideas

While the countries that the Nazis took over were run differently, some things were done the same. The Nazis tried to introduce their ideas everywhere. They were most successful in Germany itself. They had more difficulty in countries that had a long history as independent countries, such as Denmark and France. Even then, their success varied. There was a larger group of **anti-Semitic** people in France than in Denmark, for instance, so these people were more likely to accept Nazi anti-Semitism. However, this acceptance did not mean the French were more likely to accept Nazi rule. Their resistance movements fought German **occupation** just as fiercely as the Danish resistance.

Heil Hitler!

This photo shows part of a crowd at a Nazi rally in Germany in 1938. They are shouting "Heil Hitler!" and giving the Nazi salute. Hitler and the Nazis demanded that people accept and obey Nazi ideals. They called it *gleichschaltung*, meaning that everyone looked at life in the same way.

The Family

The Nazis saw families as important. They thought that men should work and fight, and women should care for the home and raise many strong, healthy children. This photograph shows an "ideal" Nazi family. The father is in the SS. The mother gave birth to many children, both girls and boys. Everyone is healthy and well fed.

Obedience

The most important Nazi idea, and the one they enforced most harshly, was obedience to the state. People were constantly told that their convenience, comfort, and even safety were less important than that of Germany. As early as 1933, official Nazi documents clearly stated: "It is all very well to reward people's merits, but the welfare of the nation must come first." The Nazis expected people to make sacrifices for their country and leader. If a member of their family was not behaving properly, it was their duty to report that person to the block warden, the Nazi official in charge of their area.

The Block Warden

The Nazis clearly laid out the duties of a block warden. This description comes from the notes a Nazi official made for a lecture:

The block consists of 40 to 60 families. The most important function of a block warden is the house visit. Every house is to be visited at least once a month, so the block warden will need assistants, one for every 10 households. The block warden needs to be aware of: the political views of the family; how committed the family is to work and to the Party; any way in which the family might influence other families; the worries, wishes, and needs of the family.

Nazi Organizations

A "good German" was expected to join one of the many different **Nazi** organizations. If he or she did not, the block warden would arrive to ask why not. Not everyone wanted to join and some refused. However, "good Germans" then treated them with suspicion, which could be dangerous.

Dangerous to Joke?

An anti-Nazi joke told in Germany criticized the way that Nazi organizations took over peoples' lives:

> *"My father is in the **SA,** my elder brother is in the **SS,** my younger brother is in the Hitler Youth, my mother is in the National Socialist Women's League, and I am in the League of German Maidens."*
>
> *"But how do you ever have time to get together with all these meetings?"*
>
> *"Oh we meet once a year at the Nazi Party Rally in Nuremberg!"*

From 1940 on, the punishment for telling an anti-Nazi joke could be hanging.

Propaganda

The Nazis believed that they would have to enforce their ideas at first, but that eventually people would follow them on their own. They used **propaganda** to make this happen. They made sure that the only ideas that were discussed on radio or in newspapers and magazines were Nazi ideas. They put up posters everywhere pushing their ideas. Irene Gut Opdyke, a young Polish nurse, remembers the German arrival in Radom, Poland:

> *Posters were pasted to the walls—cruel, mocking posters—linking the **Jews** to every sin. All the troubles of the Poles were laid at their feet. Loudspeakers on street corners blared warnings about the Jews in Polish and German.*

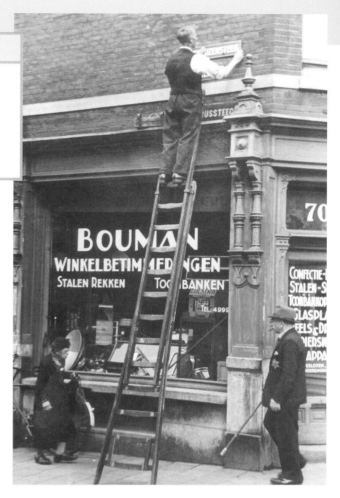

Taking Over Other Countries

The Nazis used **blitzkrieg** tactics because speed was important in invading a country. If they attacked swiftly, the army had to do less fighting because the other countries were slower to gather their armies. Less fighting for the German army meant fewer German casualties and less use of war supplies. Once the army had taken over a country, the **Gestapo** and SS arrived to keep control. The Nazis found that the quicker they took over, the better. People were still shocked and had little time to organize resistance. Tomi Ungerer, now a writer and illustrator, was a boy when the Germans took over Alsace:

The Germans didn't just arrive; they marched in, closely followed by their field kitchen. It was so quick. The French soldiers stationed in Logelbach vanished overnight and the Germans marched in. In the nearest town, Colmar, the commander of the invading unit at once demanded 2,300 kg [5,000 pounds] of bread, 557 kg [1,200 pounds] of sausages, 290 kg [640 pounds] of butter, 7 kg [15.5 pounds] of tea, 23 kg [50 pounds] of coffee, 290 liters [76.5 gallons] of rum, 23,000 packets of cigarettes, and 20 civil servants as hostages.

"Germanization"

One result of the Nazi takeover was the "Germanization" of the country. Local people soon found that they had to learn German, fast. They needed it to be able to deal with German officials and police—German speakers were more likely to be seen as "useful." Even people sent to **concentration camps** found that speaking German was helpful. German speakers were more likely to get an "easy" job in a camp office. Germanization did not just involve making the locals learn the German language. Street names were translated into German and German laws were quickly introduced.Germans also sought out people of "good" racial stock to "Germanize."

Working for Germany

All of the countries in the German **Reich** were expected to produce goods and raw materials for Germany first and their own people second. Hitler made it quite clear in several speeches and conversations that: "It is impossible for Germany to produce everything we need. So we must capture the countries with things we need, especially those things we need to continue the war." The Reich Economics Minister, Walther Funk, had to produce a plan under which Germany could take food, goods, and workers from any of the countries it controlled. In 1939, Germany had 301,000 foreign workers. This number rose rapidly. By 1944, the Reich had 7,126,000 foreign workers. This figure does not include slave labor from people in **concentration camps.**

Because **occupied** countries had to work for Germany, the country became one of the better-off European nations despite being at war. However, this improvement in the German economy came at a price.

Schemes to reduce unemployment and poverty meant that German workers were better off, but they were no longer allowed to form trade unions to protect their rights. The unemployed or homeless ended up in camps. Moreover, in the end, slave labor proved not to be very productive.

Papers

Everyone in **Nazi-**controlled lands needed documents to prove their identity and documents to prove whether or not they were **Aryan.** They needed work documents. They needed documents to travel in their own country and even more documents to leave it. Men of the right age to serve in the army needed either army documents or documents that explained why they were not in the army. All of these documents were called "**papers**" for short. Anyone could have their papers checked at any time.

Anti-Semitism

Wherever they went, the Nazis began to persecute local **Jewish** people as soon as they arrived. They put up **anti-Semitic** posters, and radios and loudspeakers churned out anti-Jewish **propaganda.** There was often very little gap between the start of German occupation and the rounding up of Jewish people to be sent to concentration camps.

The Germans marched into Alsace in France on June 17, 1940. They took control and began to spread Nazi ideas at once. One of their first propaganda moves was against Jewish people. Many Jews had decided to leave Alsace as soon as the Germans moved in. Those who moved quickly got away to safety. Those who tried to sell their homes, and make other arrangements that took time, were not so lucky. By July 16, 1940, the Nazis were ready to make Alsace *Judenfrei.* Notices appeared telling all Jews to pack a suitcase and enough food for five days. They were to be sent to France, to temporary **transit camps**, before being sent to camps in Eastern Europe. They were allowed to take 2,000 francs with them, but no jewelry—not even wedding rings.

Life in Hitler's Europe

Life across Hitler's Europe had a pattern of Nazi control. However, different people led very different lives. How rich or what race a person was, the country he or she lived in, even the ability to speak German—all of these things affected people's lives. Two workers in a factory with similar lives before the Nazis came to power could have very different lives after, especially if one was Jewish. If the non-Jew was a "good German," who believed in Nazi ideas, his living conditions might well improve under the Nazis. His Jewish co-worker would be lucky to survive Nazi rule.

Local Differences

One of the biggest differences in the way that countries pulled into the Reich reacted to Nazi ideas was in how they persecuted Jewish people. In Hungary, most persecution of Jews was done by Arrow-Cross Party "officers," as shown here. The Arrow Cross was a Hungarian organization that held many of the same beliefs as the Nazi Party.

Life for Children

The **Nazis** thought children were very important—they were the future. So, the Nazis tried to make sure that all children in the **Reich** learned to love Adolf Hitler and the Nazi state. Even coloring books for pre-school children included the **swastika** symbol.

Schools

The Nazis wanted schools to teach children how to be good Nazis. The Minister of Education said: "The whole aim of education is to create Nazis." The first step was to make sure all teachers were good Nazis. Unreliable teachers, who did not support Nazi ideas, were fired. Teachers were forced to join the National Socialist Teachers' League if they wanted to keep their jobs.

The National Socialist Teacher's League held regular Teachers' Camps on what to teach and how to teach it. Children, the League said: "must no longer be allowed to choose how to grow up. They must be taught the ideas we know to be right: the ideas of National Socialism." The Nazis decided what subjects would be taught in schools and chose the textbooks. All of this made it almost impossible for teachers to do anything but teach Nazi **propaganda** or stop teaching altogether.

School Curriculum

Schools were supposed to make sure that children grew into the kind of people the Nazis wanted. So school subjects, and their importance in the schedule, were tied to producing good soldiers, workers, and mothers. The schedule below shows a typical week's classes at a girls' school in Nazi Germany.

Periods	Monday	Tuesday	Wednesday	Thursday	Friday	Saturday
8:00–8:45	German	German	German	German	German	German
8:50–9:35	Geography	History	Singing	Geography	History	Singing
9:40–10:25	Race Study	Race Study	Race Study	Ideology	Ideology	Ideology
10:25–11:00	Recess, with sports and special announcements					
11:00–12:05	Domestic science with mathematics, every day					
12:10–12:55	Eugenics or Health Biology, alternating					

Jew Free Schools

At first, **Jewish** children were allowed to stay in ordinary schools, although they were bullied and used as "teaching aids" in race studies. Ursula Rosenfeld, a Jewish girl living in a small town near Hamburg, Germany, remembers:

> *Suddenly, no one would share a desk with me. I had to sit in a corner, at the back, on my own. When they had race studies I had to stand outside in the corridor. When I went back into class I could feel the tension. Everyone was staring, looking at you as if you were vermin.*

Jewish children and teachers were soon banned from ordinary schools. This picture from a children's book shows a Jewish teacher and Jewish students being thrown out of a school to make it **Judenfrei**—Jew free.

Shaping Minds

The Nazis were not concerned about giving children a good education. They wanted them to be turned into good Nazis. Teachers made it clear even to the youngest children that their first duty was to the state. If, for instance, children suspected anyone in their family of being anti-Nazi, they had to report them at once. Teachers also had to teach new subjects covering Nazi ideas that were clearly wrong. So, school schedules now had subjects like "race studies," which taught children that the people of the world were divided into racial groups, depending on who their ancestors were long ago, and that Germans belonged to the best race, the **Aryan** race. There was a lot more physical education (gym) to make sure everyone was fit and healthy. Girls had a lot of domestic science classes in their schedules. These classes taught them to cook, iron, and take care of babies.

Propaganda in Schools

Children were bombarded with Nazi propaganda, even in ordinary subjects at school, like math and science. Here is a question from a math textbook (RM = **Reichmarks,** German money):

> *It costs 4 RM a day to keep a mentally ill person. A civil servant earns 4 RM a day. There are at least 300,000 people in mental asylums at the moment.*
>
> *a) How much do they cost the state each day?*
>
> *b) How many marriage loans* [money the government lent to "good Germans" to marry and set up a home] *of 1,000 RM could the government pay out each day if they did not have to care for the mentally ill?*

Youth Groups

The **Nazis** also set up various **Hitler Youth** groups for children to join. They were divided up by sex and age. (There were boys groups and girls groups, for ages 10 to 14 and 14 to 18.) All of the groups stressed loyalty to the state and Adolf Hitler and provided lots of physical exercise, competition, and patriotic singing. These groups held meetings after school, in the evenings, and on weekends. They also took children on trips, usually walking and camping out. By the end of 1933, about a third of all German children aged 10 to 18 were in the Hitler Youth.

Tightening Their Hold

At first, children did not have to join Hitler Youth groups. After 1936, pressure to join increased; almost two-thirds of children had joined by the end of 1937. In 1939 a law was passed saying that children had to join. If they did not , their parents were fined or put in prison. In countries that Germany took over in Western Europe, children could not go to school unless they were members of the Hitler Youth.

Getting Used to a Uniform

The Nazis insisted that all children in Hitler Youth groups wear a uniform like this one and learn to obey orders. It was especially important for boys, as later they were expected to serve in the army. Nazi posters from the time (behind the uniform) made this connection clear.

The Hitler Youth Promise

The Hitler Youth Promise talked about Hitler, who was the Führer (leader), and the **Reich** in an almost religious way. This was not accidental. The Nazis wanted people to follow Hitler and believe in him as if he were a god:

> *You,* Führer, *are our commander!*
> *We stand in your name.*
> *The Reich is what we fight for,*
> *It is the beginning and the Amen.*
>
> *Your word is the heartbeat of our deeds;*
> *Your faith builds cathedrals for us.*
> *And even when death reaps*
> *   the last harvest*
> *The crown of the Reich never falls.*
>
> *We are ready, your silent spell*
> *Makes us one, forms us into*
> *An iron chain, man beside man,*
> *Into a wall of loyalty around you.*

Young Resistance

The Nazis were concerned about groups like the Edelweiss Pirates and the Navajo gang that actively fought Hitler Youth groups. Once Germany was at war and the Hitler Youth gave up almost all activities for military training, more young people left the Hitler Youth and joined other groups. One Edelweiss Pirate said: "It was the Hitler Youth's own fault I left. It changed so all we did was march and every order I was given came with a threat."

Once war broke out, some gangs also worked with resistance movements to fight the Nazis and help Allied troops and people who had escaped from prisons, camps, and ghettos to get out of German-controlled land. The photo shows older members of the Edelweiss Pirates group in Cologne who were caught helping resistance movements. The Nazis hanged anyone found helping anti-Nazi groups, no matter how young they were.

All in Favor?

Even inside Germany itself there were some young people who did not join the Hitler Youth. Some even formed groups opposing Nazi ideas. Groups called swing groups listened to American music and dressed very casually. This might not sound like much of a rebellion, but in Nazi Germany it was a crime. As fast as the Nazis stamped out groups, new groups sprang up. In 1942, the Reich Youth Leadership admitted: "The formation of groups of young people outside the Hitler Youth has been increasing since the outbreak of war." The most worrying thing for the Nazis was that, by 1942, nearly all of the young people had been through the Nazi school system. Yet there were still some who did not blindly accept Nazi beliefs. This meant that Nazi **propaganda** was clearly not a total success.

Playtime

The Nazis encouraged different roles for men and women. They thought men should work to earn a living and serve as soldiers. Women were expected to stay at home, look after the family and house, and have lots of children. So, children were encouraged to play with the "right sort" of toys. Girls were given tea sets, dolls, and baby buggies to practice being housewives. Boys played with toy soldiers, like the one shown here, to prepare them for when they became soldiers.

German Families

School and youth groups took up a lot of children's time, but they still had some family life. The **Nazis** encouraged big families. They also encouraged extended families, in which grandparents lived with their children's family. The extended family stressed the importance of a person's ancestors, to remind children of how important it was to come from a long line of people with "pure" German blood.

Large Families

The Nazis wanted "good Germans" to have a lot of children and to settle in the countries Germany was taking over and Germanize them. The Nazis lent suitable couples 1,000 **Reichmarks (RM)** when they married to help set up a home. The Nazis cut the loan by 250 RM for every child they had. Having four children meant the parents had nothing to repay.

The Nazis also cut taxes for large families and gave them cheap train fares, school fees, and vacations. This help was not given to families outside Germany. It had the effect the Nazis wanted. More people married and families got bigger. Children in Nazi Germany were likely to have many brothers and sisters.

A Busy Life

The Nazis saw spending time alone as **asocial.** Children in German families were encouraged to lead busy lives. They were either in school, or **kindergarten** for those under six years old, or at youth group meetings. Youth groups also organized other activities, such as collecting money for charities. Children had to help in the home, too. This help depended on their age and where they lived. Farmers' children helped on the farm beginning at a very young age.

Families Outside Germany

Families outside Germany were not treated as well as "good German" families, but they did not have to follow as many rules either. Women were discouraged from working and children were expected to join **Hitler Youth** groups. Otherwise, family life could carry on as normal, as long as people obeyed the new Nazi laws. Children from families the Nazis saw as asocial or **undesirable** were either taken away from their parents or sent with them to **concentration camps.**

Unwanted Children

When the Nazis imprisoned and killed **Jewish** people, babies, young children, and pregnant mothers were among the first to die. This was partly because they could not work efficiently. It was also because children were the next generation—they gave people hope and carried on a race that the Nazis wanted to wipe out. Disabled German children were also killed. Women considered unsuitable as mothers because of their race or a disability were operated on to keep them from having children.

"Aryanizing" Children

When the Nazis took over Poland, they took young Polish children that looked Aryan away from their parents. They sent the children to be adopted by German families who could not have children. The Nazis thought that with "better" parents these children would become good Nazis. The younger the child, the easier it was for him or her to adapt quickly. The boy in this photo is the kind of child the Nazis chose, although his age would mean he might adapt more slowly. The Nazis did not separate families in Western Europe in this way because they saw the people in these countries as more civilized.

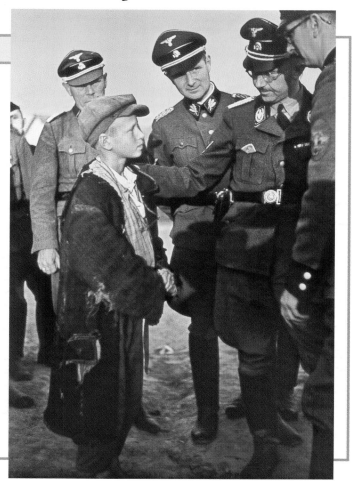

Making Friends

Making friends in Hitler's Europe was difficult. Children could not just make friends with someone they liked. Children, or their parents if they were young children, had to think about how suitable another child was. It was dangerous to be friends with the wrong people. It was especially dangerous for children with something to hide. If a child was **Jewish,** but pretending not to be, or if a child's parents were working against the **Nazis,** it was dangerous to make friends with someone from a Nazi family. Children did not always understand that if they said something to the wrong person it could be a disaster. Christabel Bielenberg, an Englishwoman living in Nazi Germany, remembers:

My son, Nicky, came home from school one day after playing with his friend Werner. "Do you know Werner's mother listens to the radio like you do, with her ear right up against it?" he asked. [This meant she was listening to a banned radio station—a crime that earned at least five years in prison and could get a person hung.] "She's probably a bit deaf, like me," I said firmly.

Safety in Numbers

Children in Nazi Germany were encouraged to make large groups of friends in their **Hitler Youth** groups. These friendships were less deep and less likely to affect a child's loyalty to the Nazis. These girls are at a Hitler Youth camp for 14 to18 year olds.

Losing Old Friends

Once the Nazis came to power, many Jewish children found that it was hard to stay friends with non-Jews. Anne Fox, a Jewish girl living in Berlin, remembers the effect of the Nazis coming to power on her friendships:

*My friend Tuke, who lived in the same apartment block, came to play less and less often. My mother didn't like me going up to their apartment, either. Tuke's older brother, Hans, was in the **SA** and her father was one of the first to join the **SS.** The boys marched and sang, with all the other Nazis: "When Jewish blood spurts from the knife, how much better everything will be!" How could a friendship cope with that?*

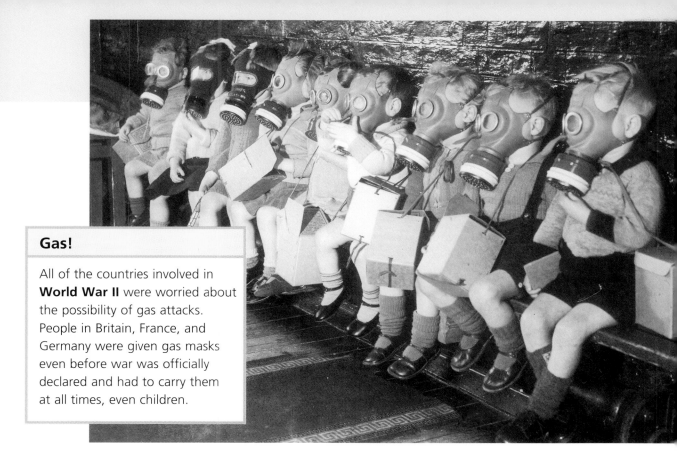

Gas!

All of the countries involved in **World War II** were worried about the possibility of gas attacks. People in Britain, France, and Germany were given gas masks even before war was officially declared and had to carry them at all times, even children.

War!

Germany was at war with various other countries from 1939 to 1945, including Britain and France from 1939, and the Soviet Union and the United States from 1941. War affected all of the children living in Germany and **occupied** Europe. Many German families were broken up as fathers and elder brothers had to join the army. Many city children were sent away from their homes when bombing raids on Germany began. They did not have to go, but there was a lot of pressure on parents to send their children. They were safer in the countryside, but it was another change to get used to. Children aged 6 to 10 were sent to live with families. Children aged 10 to 14 were sent to live in state-organized hostels or campsites.

Rationing

The Nazis rationed food, gasoline, and clothes beginning in August 1939, the month before war broke out. Rationing meant Germans were only allowed a certain amount of each of these things. Often, it was not nearly as much as people had been used to. Children in all of the countries at war were affected by shortages of food and other everyday things.

Starving in the Ghettos

Jewish children who were rounded up with their families into **ghettos** suffered from rationing more than other children. The Nazis only let a small amount of food into the ghettos—less than enough to keep everyone alive. People died every day in each ghetto from starvation.

23

Life for Women

The **Nazis** had strong ideas about the role of women. They wanted women to marry, run the home, and have lots of children. They did not want women, especially married women, to work. As the war took away more and more men to fight, the Nazis had to change their views about working women. They had to ask women to do war work for their country. They made it clear that they wanted this to be a temporary, emergency change.

Bombing

This photo shows women clearing away the rubble in Berlin after a British bombing raid in 1945. The British and Germans bombed each other's cities heavily between 1941 and 1945. Hermine Jundt, a young mother living in Mannheim, wrote to a friend:

> Things are so awful here now, Anna. Thirteen bombs dropped near us. They've made huge craters and the dirt and rubble are awful. When we got home from the shelter I wanted to howl. No lights, no water, no gas! I didn't know where to begin. Over 180,000 firebombs were dropped on the town, so you can imagine that the fires were burning for days on end.

Raising a Family

Hitler said in a speech in 1934: "Equal rights for women means valuing them for the job nature has given them." He believed that men and women were made differently and had different skills. Both sets of skills were needed for a state to work well. One of the jobs only women could do was having babies and raising the next generation of German **citizens.** So, mothers were valued. Mothers in Nazi Germany were given extra rations and were even given medals for having a lot of healthy babies. Anna Klein, a young German mother who lived in Vienna, remembers:

> Ever since I was little all I had wanted was to be a mother and have lots of babies. I really fit Hitler's image of the perfect German mother. I felt lucky to be a mother then, too. I was treated as if I was special, not like my mother and aunties had been— they didn't get all those extras.

Feeding a Family

Feeding a family became harder and harder with wartime rationing, especially in the cities. People had coupons that they swapped for their rations, as shown in the photograph. However, just because people had the coupons did not mean that they got the food. One woman remembered:

You spent all morning shopping for food. The queues [lines] were terrible. And you had to queue [line up] over and over, for each thing, bread, meat, groceries. It could be heartbreaking. Sometimes, if you were late getting to the shops, the shopkeepers ran out just as you got to the front of the queue [line], over and over.

Women living in the countryside could keep hens for eggs and to eat when they stopped laying. Some local farmers sold or swapped spare milk, butter, or cheese.

Foreign Women

Non-German women living in Germany were treated with suspicion. Christabel Bielenberg, an Englishwoman married to a German, found that she was treated with suspicion in Berlin, but people were more friendly when she moved to the countryside. The Nazis did not force the women of **occupied** Europe to behave like German women, but they did not give them any of the benefits, either.

A Different Attitude?

Many women who worked in resistance movements remembered that it was an advantage being a woman, especially a pretty young woman. A Polish resister remembers: "I smiled and flirted with the Nazi guards. These were my weapons." They deliberately tried to fit the Nazi image and used this to appear invisible. It did not help them if they were caught helping the resistance, though. They were hung.

Working Life

Before the **Nazis** took over, Germany, like much of the rest of Europe, had serious economic problems. High unemployment and rising prices made it hard for many people to make a living.

Improvements

The Nazis took jobs away from **Jews** and women and gave them to "suitable" unemployed German men. The next unemployment figures did not count Jews or women—so the number dropped hugely. The Nazis set up state work projects, building roads and rebuilding cities, creating nearly 2 million more jobs for men who accepted Nazi rule. Wages began to go up, while prices stopped going up so quickly. Nazi organizations made sure working conditions were good and provided free sporting activities and cheap vacations. The Nazis also helped unemployed people who they thought were genuinely unable to work by providing for their basic needs. However, unemployed people who the Nazis thought were avoiding work were described as **asocial** and sent to the camps.

Hard Work

The Nazis believed that hard physical work was good for people and produced fit, healthy **citizens.** Young people in Nazi-controlled lands were expected to spend six months doing Labor Service as soon as they were eighteen years old. This work usually involved making roads or working on farms. These postcards show young men happily "working for Germany."

More Restrictions

Only men who accepted Nazi ideas were likely to find their working life improved. Many **undesirable** people lost their jobs under the Nazis. Also, workers could not set up their own trade unions to say what they wanted. Trade unions were banned and many of their leaders were sent to **concentration camps.** Working conditions were hard, as Ernst Bromberg, a steelworks fitter, remembers:

> *There was no time to get into politics when you were working three shifts with the Labor Front breathing down your necks. You got up, went to work, didn't overstretch your breaks and took the money. It was good money.*

Forced to Work

People in countries to the east of Germany, such as Poland, were forced to work. The Nazis classed people in these eastern countries as Slavs. To the Nazis, Slavs were *untermenschen*—less than human—so the Nazis did not treat them as if they had human rights. If the Nazis in Radom, Poland, for instance, needed workers for a factory, they simply went out with trucks and loaded up healthy-looking Poles from the street. These people were not allowed to collect any things or to tell their families they were going. Irene Gut Opdyke, a young Polish girl, was taken from a church in Radom:

> *The soldiers began dividing people up and I was dragged to a group of "fit workers." Three trucks roared into the church square and we were chased into them. We were driven to some kind of*

> *camp, surrounded by barbed wire. "You will be taken to Germany to work for the **Reich**," an officer told us. "You Poles have been idle long enough."*

Germany First

Workers in **occupied** Western Europe were not as badly treated as in Eastern Europe, but they still had to put Germany first. Despite claiming that all of the countries were working for a common goal, the Nazis were actually exploiting Europe. Farmers had their food taken to feed the German army. Factories were re-equipped to make ammunition and other goods for Germany's war.

Leisure Time

The **Nazis** wanted people to work hard for Hitler and Germany. By the time they had done their work and gone to all of the meetings of groups they had to join, people had very little free time left. However, the Nazis encouraged suitable group entertainment, which they used to spread Nazi **propaganda.** They built theaters to show Nazi-approved movies and plays. The Nazis also made cheap radios and gave many of them away to poor families who would otherwise not be able to afford one. Free radios meant that, as a poster of the time said: "Everyone listens to the *Führer* on National Radio!"

The 1936 Olympic Games

In 1936 Germany hosted the Olympic Games. Hitler had a brand new Olympic Stadium built for the Games. It was the Nazis' chance to show the world how civilized they were, how much better their **Aryan** athletes were than other athletes. The streets were cleaned of their most violent anti-**Jewish** posters and obvious violence against Jews and other **undesirables** was discouraged. It was a great humiliation for Hitler to watch while an African-American athlete, Jesse Owens, won four gold medals, beating Aryan athletes. Hitler ignored Owens and walked out when the crowd stood to cheer his win in the 200 meter sprint. Out of 129 events, Germany won only 33 gold medals.

Culture

Hermann Goering, a member of the Nazi Party and a close friend of Hitler, summed up many Nazis' attitude when he said: "Whenever I hear the word 'culture' I reach for my revolver." However, Hitler wanted the world to see the Nazis as cultured, not as thugs. So, the Nazis supported painters, musicians, writers, and playwrights—as long as they supported Nazi ideas. Other artists were seen as **degenerate** and their works were banned. The last thing the Nazis wanted was people being encouraged to think for themselves. They held regular public burnings of degenerate books. The first of these was on May 10, 1933, after the Nazis had been in power for less than four months.

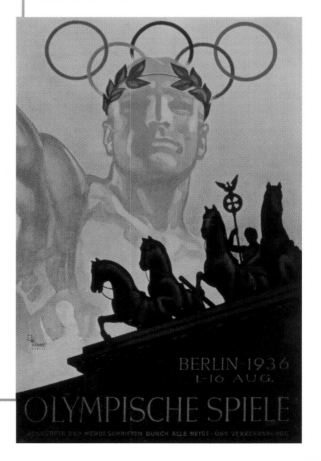

A Fan of Mickey Mouse

Hitler saw his first Mickey Mouse cartoon in 1937. He loved it so much that the propaganda minister, Joseph Goebbels, gave him twelve Mickey cartoons for Christmas. Goebbels set up a team of over 100 cartoonists to study and copy Disney's techniques to make propaganda films such as *The Jewish Rhinoceros*, a frame of which is shown here. In it, a Jewish rhinoceros exploits all of the other animals for his own profit and has to be defeated. Goebbels wanted to be able to use the films to spread propaganda in any country that Germany took over, subtitling them in a variety of languages.

Shakespeare—a Good German?

The Nazis tried to prove that anyone who had invented anything useful, or written or composed anything important, was really German. The English playwright, William Shakespeare, had been important in Germany for many years. The Nazis did not want to ban Shakespeare at once, for fear of upsetting too many people. Instead they had editions of his plays "re-edited" to smooth away anything anti-Nazi. The Ministry of Propaganda even wrote a pamphlet called *Shakespeare—a Germanic Writer*. Then, in 1939, Germany went to war with Britain and all "enemy dramatists" were banned. Hitler, who liked Shakespeare, said he was not banned. So Nazi propaganda showed Shakespeare as a writer only Germans understood—the British were too stupid: "The only Shakespeare known in England today is a football player of that name." However, one by one the plays came to be seen as unacceptable. In the end, the Nazis put so many restrictions on which plays could be performed, and how many times, that they might as well have banned them.

Undermining Religion, Creating Suspicion

Hitler realized that the **Nazis** could not just ban all religions. Too many people had sincerely held beliefs for banning to have any chance of success. So when the Nazis came to power, Hitler was friendly to the Christian Church. He even made an agreement with the Pope that the Nazis would not interfere with the Catholic Church as long as the Pope did not interfere in German politics.

Undermining the Churches

However, Hitler secretly worked against the Catholic Church, which said Catholics should obey the Pope before the ruler of their country. The Nazis never banned the Catholic Church, but they persecuted Catholic priests. They set up the "German Christian Church," with the aim of: "embracing all the people into a National Socialist State. . . . One Nation! One God! One **Reich**! One Church!" They also encouraged "nature worship". So, instead of celebrating Easter, they held a pagan spring festival to undermine the traditional Christian festival. Outside Germany, the Nazis allowed Christians to go on worshiping in their own way.

The Jewish Faith

There was one religion the Nazis never tolerated—the **Jewish** faith. Jewish synagogues were often targets of Nazi violence. On the night of November 9, 1938, the Nazis carried out a planned, countrywide attack against Jews. It was known as *Kristallnacht* (Night of Broken Glass) because of all the damage done. Over a thousand synagogues were burned down and many more were looted. Eric Lucas, a Jewish boy living in Aachen, remembers:

> *Three men threw the scrolls of the Law of Moses* [part of the Jewish sacred writings] *to the screaming mass of people. The people caught the scrolls and tossed them as if playing a ball game. They were torn and trampled.*

30

Moving Around

Under the Nazis it was not possible for anyone to move around freely, especially after war broke out in 1939. Walking and bicycling short distances were the quickest ways to get around, although a person might have to show his or her **papers** at any time. Train travel required a permit and was likely to be difficult and dangerous during the war.

"Suspicious" People

The Nazis encouraged people to report anyone "suspicious" who might, for instance, be listening to British radio broadcasts or hiding Jewish families. The Nazis were quick to imprison people, especially foreign men, for any reason. Foreigners who had a job where they could pass on anti-Nazi views were almost automatically seen as opponents and arrested, as in the case of Stefan Lorant. Before the war, if these people were lucky, they simply went to prison until they could be sent out of Germany. After the war had started they were sent to **concentration camps.**

Stefan Lorant—Under Arrest

Stefan Lorant was a Hungarian filmmaker and photographer. He was arrested in Munich on March 14, 1933, just five days after the Nazis took over in Bavaria. He was kept in prison in Munich for six and a half months, and constantly shifted from cell to cell. He was always afraid he might be executed or sent to a concentration camp, as other **politicals** had been. The worst thing was the uncertainty. Eventually the Hungarian embassy managed to get him released. He was given a day to leave the country and return to Hungary. In Britain, in 1935, he published his book, *I Was Hitler's Prisoner*. In this book he said:

> *For six and a half months I was in* **"protective custody"** *as a political offender. Why? I was never told. My case never came to trial. My wife, by trying to get me released, upset the political police. She was imprisoned for six and a half weeks, also with no explanation and no trial.*

Life in the Ghettos

Ghettos were places, usually parts of cities or towns in **occupied** countries, where the **Nazis** forced **Jewish** people to live. Cramming Jews into ghettos made the rest of the city and the land around it *Judenfrei*—Jew free. The first ghetto was set up in Piotrkow, Poland, in October 1939. Gradually, ghettos were set up in many other cities. The largest of these were in Warsaw and Lodz.

A Good Thing?

At first, many Jewish people welcomed the setting up of ghettos. There were several reasons. Ghettos had been set up as early as medieval times, so they were familiar. The people in these early ghettos had lived separately, but they had still lived normal lives. They had been allowed to move around outside the ghettos and do business with non-Jews. Jews in Nazi Germany hoped that the Nazi ghettos would work in the same way. Also, persecution was less obvious at first, because there was less contact with non-Jews. It looked as though things would settle down, not get worse. Everyone in the ghetto was Jewish, and a *Judenrat*, Jewish Council, was set up to run things. Jewish people would be cut off from the outside world but running things for themselves.

It soon became clear that the Nazi's ghettos would not be like earlier ones. The Nazi ghettos were walled and guarded parts of cities and towns into which Jews, first from the Polish countryside and then from Germany and other lands occupied by Germany, were crammed.

The Warsaw Ghetto

This photograph was taken in the Warsaw ghetto in 1940, not long after the ghetto had been set up. The streets are crowded, but people are still reasonably well fed and do not yet look like they are starving.

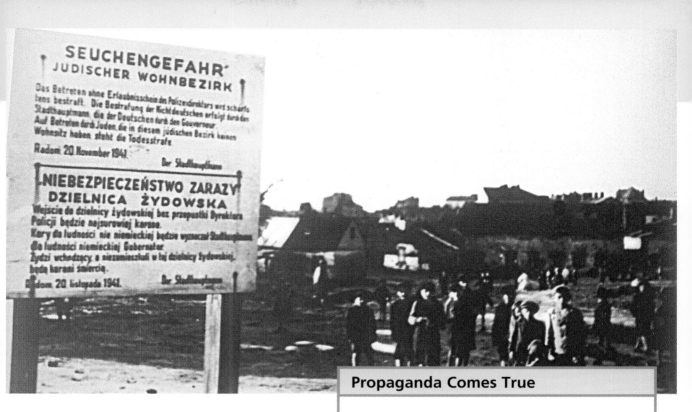

All Together

In the ghettos a lot of people were crammed into a small area—and their numbers rose as the Nazis rounded up more and more Jews. About 500,000 people were forced into the Warsaw ghetto. Despite the fact that they died at rates that varied from 1,000 to 6,000 a month, the ghetto population rose as the Nazis crammed more and more Jews from Germany, occupied Europe, and Poland into it. The same thing happened in the other ghettos.

The advantages that many Jews had hoped for did not happen. The *Judenrat* had to obey the Nazis, so Jews were not running their own lives. The ghetto held Jewish people in one place, so the Nazis knew just where to find them to persecute them. The Nazis regularly cut off water and electricity, using the excuse of wartime rationing. They also limited supplies of food and medicine.

Propaganda Comes True

This photo shows the entrance to the Jewish ghetto in Radom. The notice outside warns against entry "because of disease." By cramming people into the ghettos the way they did, with limited access to water, medicine, heat, and electricity, the Nazis made sure that their **propaganda** about Jews being dirty and carrying diseases came true. People in the ghetto made huge efforts to stay clean and to help the sick, but they were fighting such terrible conditions that they were sure to lose.

In 1941 the ration for a German adult was 2,613 calories (approximately the recommended daily calorie intake today). Poles were only allowed 699 calories. Jews in the ghettos got 184 calories—well below the amount needed to survive. The overcrowding and lack of water, heat, and light soon led to the rapid spread of disease.

33

Isolated

Because **Jewish** people were cut off in **ghettos,** it was easy for the **Nazis** to persecute them and for the people outside the ghetto to ignore it. The Nazis were forcing people in the ghetto to live in appalling conditions—but they exaggerated even these conditions to make Jewish people seem inhuman. The **SS** paper, *Das Schwarze Korps*, said in an article on ghettos in 1939:

> *The ghetto is unbelievably filthy, a maze of alleys and overfilled buildings, full of Jews whose numbers increase rapidly, despite poverty and typhus. Countless habitual criminals, murderers, swindlers, and pickpockets hide here—they have to be cleared out of their underground rats' nests by German cleaning crews at the risk of their own lives. This clearing strains the nerves of the men who have to fight through the stench, muck, muck, and more muck, through vermin-infested and disgusting Jewish living spaces.*

Work Break

These Jewish workers in the Lodz ghetto have stopped for a meal break. The factories fed the workers a thin soup in the middle of the day. It was often the only food they had all day, despite the heavy work and long hours.

Inequality in the Ghetto

Not everyone in the ghetto was equal. Members of the *Judenrat* and Jews who had been wealthy before the Nazi occupation lived far better than other people. People who ran the ghetto workshops also had better lives. They had their own apartments with electricity and running water, rather than having to share. They were also given more food.

The poor people sent to the ghetto well after the ghetto was set up were the worst off. They lived in the poorest parts of the ghetto, with several families forced to share a single room that had no water, heat, or electricity.

Deportations

In 1942 the Nazis decided that it was not enough for Jews to be left in the ghettos to die of disease and starvation. It was not even enough to put them in the camps and work them to death. Special **death camps** were set up to do nothing but kill Jewish people and other **undesirables,** such as the gypsies.

Jews in the ghetto were ferried to these camps by train, having been told they would be resettled outside German land. It was suspicious that the first to go were the very young, the old, the sick, and the pregnant—not healthy people who could have set up a settlement. As trainload after trainload of people left, and small ghettos were "liquidated," it became harder to believe that the trains were taking people to anything but their death. People in the ghettos began to revolt against the Nazis.

The Terezín Ghetto

In October 1941, the Nazis decided to turn the walled town of Terezín, in Czechoslovakia, into a ghetto. They moved all the non-Jewish people out and, over the next few months, moved about 40,000 Jewish people in. Terezín was unusual in that the Nazis used it as a "model" ghetto to show that conditions in ghettos were not bad. They filmed it in 1944 and even showed members of the Red Cross charity organization around it, having first carried out an "improvement action" to make it look far better than it was. An SS man drove the leader of the *Judenrat*, Paul Eppstein, around the ghetto in a car. The same SS man had beaten Eppstein up the day before, and would do so again.

An Unknown Destination

These people are being loaded onto trains leaving the Lodz ghetto in the summer of 1944. They were told they were being sent to settle lands farther east, setting up new Jewish communities. In fact, they were being sent to death camps.

The Lodz Ghetto

The Lodz **ghetto** was set up in April 1940. The **Jewish** people of Lodz hardly fit into the ghetto, let alone all of the people from the nearby countryside, too. In the first month or so about 38,000 Jews were sent to Lodz. Jews from all over Europe were crammed in. Meanwhile, as disease and starvation took hold, the death rate of the people in the ghetto rose rapidly.

Outside Contacts

People in other ghettos had some outside contact and some managed to smuggle in money, food, or news. Irene Gut Opdyke, a young Polish girl, worked close enough to the Radom ghetto to be able to slip away and sneak food under the ghetto fence each day. On the other hand, the Lodz ghetto was completely cut off. There were factories inside the Lodz ghetto, so Jews did not leave the ghetto to work. More importantly, the **Nazis** filled the area around the ghetto with people from Germany, **Aryans** who had no connection with, or sympathy for, the people inside.

Jewish Cemetery

Jewish Cemetery

Cemetery

Catholic Cemetery

Park

Catholic Cemetery

Park

Park

Park

Cemetery

Park

Park

Park

Park

Catholic Cemetery

Park

Catholic Cemetery

Park

0   2000 yards

0   2000 m

–·–·– City boundary

– – – Ghetto boundary

⬛ Ghetto area

The Lodz Ghetto

The Lodz ghetto was fenced off with 6.82 miles (eleven kilometers) of barbed wire fence. There were narrow wooden bridges over the "Aryan" streets. There were 31,721 apartments, most of them with only one room and only 725 with running water. Few had electricity. At its fullest, there were over 200,000 people living there.

Finding Out About the Lodz Ghetto

Survivors from Lodz have talked about their experiences of ghetto life. Also, the *Judenrat* (Jewish Council) that ran the ghetto kept a secret diary of events: *Chronicle of the Lodz Ghetto*. It was written by several people, intended to record exactly what went on. This is the only surviving day-to-day account of events in a ghetto.

The Nazis did not know about the *Chronicle*. The Nazis would have hung the writers, even though they only put down the facts. They did not criticize either the Nazis or the *Judenrat* (whose decisions were not always popular). There are also photos of the ghetto—some taken publicly by Nazi officers and some taken secretly by Jewish photographers.

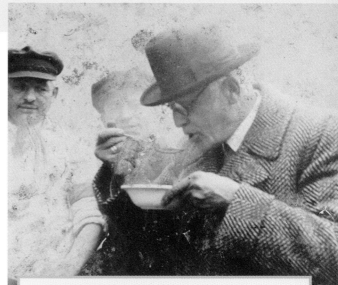

Mordecai Chaim Rumkowski

This photo shows Mordecai Rumkowski, the leader of the *Judenrat*, at the opening of a new soup kitchen in the Lodz ghetto. Rumkowski was the most well-off man in the ghetto and was often called "the king."

Running the Ghetto

Mordecai Chaim Rumkowski was the leader of the *Judenrat* that ran the Lodz ghetto. He was convinced that the way to survive in the ghetto was to cooperate with the Nazis and show that they were useful. He was sure that if the Jews of the ghetto worked hard for the Nazis they would be allowed to live. He set up offices to run the work, the rationing, schools (Lodz was one of the few ghettos that managed to keep schools going), emergency services, and all kinds of welfare. The welfare department organized soup kitchens in various areas and did what they could to look after the poor, old, sick, and orphans. On August 4, 1944, Mordecai Rumkowski and his family were deported to Auschwitz and killed.

Desperation

Even during the first winter, the lack of food and fuel made people desperate. Coal dust was sold for fuel, while people used whatever they could get as firewood. While some people went out of their way to help others, many people, not surprisingly, put their families first. If they had to steal, they stole. In January 1941, the *Chronicle* reported:

The residents of a building woke today to find that they could not go downstairs. During the night someone had stolen the stairs, banisters, and handrail.

Work in the Ghetto

Everyone in the **ghetto** worked if they could, for as long as they could. People who worked were fed a meal at their job. Even people who had been doctors or teachers were glad to work many hours a day sweeping floors or clearing rubble.

Good Jobs?

Some people were lucky enough to get work running the ghetto. This entitled a person to two bowls of soup a day, not the one that all other workers got. Michael Etkind was a postman in Lodz and remembers that even on two bowls of soup, he was constantly hungry:

> *We all were. Rations were given out every two weeks. Many people could not stop themselves [from] eating it too quickly. So it was gone by the middle of the second week. So they were so hungry that when the next distribution of bread and butter came they would eat it all too quickly again.*

Some "official" jobs gave the worker extra rations, but made him unpopular, especially working as a ghetto police officer. The ghetto police had to keep people from leaving the ghetto, carry out **Nazi** orders, and break up the rioting that broke out when conditions were especially bad.

Taken Away to Work

The Nazis regularly took trainloads of the fittest in the ghetto, usually men, to do forced labor, usually in Germany. They did this before they started deporting people to **concentration camps** and to **death camps**. On April 11, 1941, they announced that they would take 300 or 400 workers every three or four days for the rest of the month. These men never returned to their families in the ghetto.

Making Things Worse

The Nazis regularly made things worse in the ghettos. They might reduce the size of a ghetto while increasing the number of people. They might also cut the amount of food and medicines. In January 1941, the Nazis took a section of the Lodz ghetto away. They did not choose the particular piece of land they took by accident. Their action managed to decrease the food supply and increase overcrowding in the ghetto at the same time. The *Chronicle* reported that:

> *The 7,000 or so people from this area will have to be found somewhere to live. The loss of land is especially painful because the largest fruit and vegetable growing area is there. These were carefully begun last year on land previously used for dumping rubbish.*

Deportations

The Nazis began **deportations** from Lodz in January 1942. Many people from the Lodz ghetto were taken to Chelmno and Auschwitz-Birkenau death camps. Perec Zylberberg, a young man in the ghetto, remembers:

> *The deportations got more and more frequent. We didn't know what was wrong, but we sensed something was. The people in charge were trying so hard to save their relatives from going. I was able to get my mother and sister work at the carpet factory where I worked. Working was a passport to staying on.*

Beginning on September 5, 1942, there was a curfew in the ghetto for seven days. Factories were closed, everything stopped, and people were collected for deportation. By the end of the seventh day about 20,000 people were gone. From June to August 1944, the Lodz ghetto was emptied as its residents were transported to death camps. By the time the advancing Russian troops captured Lodz on January 19, 1945, only 870 people remained of the 230,000 in the ghetto at its fullest.

Everyone Helps

Very young children did not work in the factories, but they could still help by selling things on street corners. This boy is selling "homemade sweets."

39

Special Cases

The **Nazis** persecuted **Jewish** people the most, but there were other people who were mistreated and even killed. There were three kinds of "special cases"—people who did not fit into the perfect Nazi state. They were the disabled, the **Gypsies,** and **asocials.**

The Disabled

In August 1938, the Nazis began to encourage German people to send their disabled relatives to state-run clinics for "special care." The clinic at Eglfing-Haar near Munich was one of the first to open. Its director, Dr. Hermann Pfannmüller, showed some Nazis around the clinic in February 1940. One of them remembered:

*He took us into one ward and said: "We have here children from one to five, all living burdens on our nation. We do not poison or inject them—this might give the foreign press a **propaganda** hold against us. No, our way is much simpler." At this he pulled a skeletal child out of one of the cots saying: "Naturally we don't stop all their food at once. That would cause too much fuss. We gradually reduce the portions. Nature takes care of the rest. This one won't last more than two or three days."*

At least 5,000 children were killed in this way.

T4

The Nazis had a policy of starving disabled adults, or leaving them exposed in cold weather to freeze to death. These people were also mass-gassed by carbon monoxide in an operation code-named "T4." There were six centers for gassing, like the Hartheim Institute pictured left, scattered all over Germany. Victims' families got a letter saying the patient had fallen ill:

. . . all attempts to keep the patient alive were unfortunately unsuccessful. In accordance with police instructions we had to cremate the corpse at once to prevent spreading infectious disease.

Gypsies

Gypsies share the same language and culture. Gypsies are people who travel in groups, often on the same routes year after year, meeting up in larger groups at various times. By the 1930s, some Gypsy families had settled down to live in towns and villages. While some of these people still saw themselves as Gypsies, others did not and some married non-Gypsy people. The Nazis murdered about 300,000 Gypsies in the **Holocaust** that also wiped out millions of **Jews.** Why did the Nazis target the Gypsies?

Racially Inferior

The **SS** had orders to treat the Gypsies as if they were Jews: "to be removed from Europe as an inferior **race**." The Nazis thought it was impossible to re-educate the Gypsies into Nazi ways. Rudolf Hoess, commandant of Auschwitz **concentration camp,** showed this Nazi prejudice when he said: "Stealing and vagrancy are in their blood and cannot be wiped out." Nazi officials traced back family lines and arrested people with even a small amount of Gypsy blood. Even Nazi soldiers who did not know they had Gypsy ancestors were sent to Auschwitz.

Traveling People

This photo shows Gypsies in a camp near Hamburg in the spring of 1940. Before they were sent to their deaths, many Gypsies were sent to permanent fenced and guarded campsites like this one. The man in the suit taking notes in the middle of the group is Nazi scientist Dr. Robert Ritter, who studied **race.**

Roman Mirga

Roman Mirga's family lived in Warsaw, Poland, working in a Gypsy band. In November 1942, when Roman was 17, they were warned that the Nazis were persecuting Gypsies. The Gypsy leader did not believe they were in danger. Then a group of Gypsies vanished and Roman's group fled toward Hungary. They disguised themselves as Polish peasants. The Nazis caught some of them, but some made it, including Roman and his family. When the Germans invaded Hungary, on July 31, 1944, 4,000 people in the Gypsy camp were gassed. Roman was one of the few people who were kept as workers. Roman and another young Gypsy escaped and hid with a Polish woman until the Russians arrived in January 1945.

Asocials at Hashude

The **Nazis** wanted healthy **Aryan asocials,** especially families with children, to have a chance to reform. In October 1936 a "welfare housing institution," called Hashude, was set up in the city of Bremen. It was for "re-educating" asocial families. It looked like an ordinary housing estate, not a prison or a camp, but families were forced to go there. While there, they were constantly watched.

Constant Supervision

The estate at Hashude, shown here, was surrounded by fences and the gates were guarded. The houses had no back doors, just front doors—most of which were overlooked by the Nazi administration building. Welfare officials could go into any house at any time to check what the families were doing, how clean the houses were, and how well looked after the children were.

Who Was Sent to Hashude?

Government welfare officials decided which families were sent to Hashude. They chose families that they thought could be changed. Families were chosen if the parents did not work, drank too much, neglected the children, or did not pay the rent.

Even members of the Nazi Party could be sent to Hashude. In May 1936, a family was sent to Hashude even though the father had been a member of the Nazi party since it was set up and the children were in Nazi youth groups. The reasons given for sending them to Hashude were that the father had not paid the rent for a whole year and his wife's housekeeping showed that "the ideas of order and cleanliness were unknown to her."

A Perfect Estate?

Hashude had 84 family houses, a children's block, a bathing area, and an administration building. It was praised in an article in the **SS** magazine *Das Schwarze Korps*. The article also stressed that it was "The Last Chance" for these people before they were sent to a concentration camp. This was a fate that most people wanted to avoid.

The Routine in Hashude

In their first six months at Hashude, new families had no contact with other families. Fathers worked in local factories and workshops or did gardening and repairs in Hashude. Mothers looked after the home and children. Houses had to be cleaned by 11 A.M. each day. Welfare officers inspected homes daily, returning over and over until they were satisfied that the home was clean enough. Children had to join the **Hitler Youth**. Babies and children up to the age of six were cared for in the children's block in the morning, while their mothers cleaned and cooked. Older children went to school and then spent time in the children's block in the afternoon, learning hygiene and doing physical exercises.

More Freedom

If the welfare officials were satisfied that a family had improved after six months, they were moved to a terraced house and could spend time with other families. They had more freedom, although welfare officers could visit at any time. As soon as the officer in charge of Hashude felt that a family was no longer "a threat to the nation," he reported to the Welfare Authority that they were ready for release. The Welfare Authority then looked for a home for the family and a job for the father. The family was not allowed to leave until these were found.

Hashude Closes

In July 1940, Hashude was closed down. A housing shortage in Bremen meant that the houses were too valuable to "waste" on asocials. The fencing and gates were taken down and it re-opened as ordinary housing for families from Bremen. The Nazis had been rounding up large numbers of asocials and sending them to **concentration camps** since July 1938. With Hashude gone, there was no other alternative.

Living in Hiding

Jewish people who escaped the **ghetto** or the camps, or who never entered them, living instead in hiding, were called "submarines." Life as a submarine was very dangerous.

Papers

Everyone in Hitler's Europe needed identity documents, called papers for short. Anyone could have their **papers** checked at any time. Many submarines spent a lot of money on forged papers. Submarines had to be careful all the time. They had to remember the false names and the story they made up about their lives to go with them. They had to be very careful whom they trusted and this was hard for those who were passed along from hiding place to hiding place. Edith Hahn, a Jewish woman who survived the war pretending to be **Aryan**, remembers:

> . . . you might never use them, but you had them, you see. It gave you confidence that you were protected and that was half the battle for us submarines hiding among the enemy. If you had confidence the terror and stress of daily life would not show on your face and give you away.

Edith herself was even luckier. Her papers were actually genuine. They belonged to Christl Beran, a friend who gave Edith her papers. She told the **Nazis** she had lost the papers, and was given copies to replace them. If the Nazis had found out what Christl had done they would have almost certainly hanged her.

The Yellow Star

All **Jews** had to wear a yellow Star of David on the shoulder of their clothes. Submarines did not do this. The luckiest submarines were blonde haired and blue eyed. Nazi **propaganda** led most guards to expect Jews to have dark skin, black hair, and big noses.

The Soros Family

Tivadar Soros was a Hungarian Jew who went into hiding with his family in Budapest. They had to survive for more than ten months—Budapest was not fully liberated until February 13, 1945. In that short time, the Nazis rounded up more than half of all the Jewish people living in Hungary—about 434,000 people—and sent them to their deaths.

A Big Decision

Tivadar heard of the Nazi invasion in March 1944 on the radio. By 1944, there was no mistaking what it would mean for Hungarian Jews. Over the next few days he noticed: "The first to be caught were people trying to leave: the railway station and roads were heavily guarded." The Nazis set up a *Judenrat*, a Jewish Council, and put them "in charge" of all the Jews in the city. Within days the schools were closed. The older children ran errands for the *Judenrat*. One day George was sent to deliver notices telling people to report to a meeting point with a blanket and food for two days. The people on the list were all lawyers with surnames beginning with A, B, or C. "By the end of the week they had reached the letter G. I decided we all had to disappear."

Getting Papers

Tivadar saw that: "It was clear we would only survive if we lived as Christians. We needed new identity papers, a new apartment, and a new name." Tivadar tried to get ahold of some papers. At first, he got nowhere, but then a friend said he could get birth and marriage certificates (proving you were Aryan) and blank residence forms (to prove you lived in a particular place) with an official stamp.

Yet, Tivadar still needed personal documents—identity cards with photos, work permits, ration cards, travel permits, and military papers. Just as he was beginning to despair, both his brother and the caretaker of a building he managed gave him papers.

45

Invaded

The German army moved into Hungary with their usual speed. This photo shows a heavy tank and German soldiers in a street in Budapest in March 1944, soon after they had invaded.

Splitting Up

The Soros family faced a hard decision. Should they stay together? Tivadar decided they had a better chance of at least some of them surviving if they split up. Paul was the first to go. On his 18th birthday he was told to report to a **Jewish labor camp**. He moved out and began life as a Christian student at the university. George went to live with a Mr. Baufluss, who worked for the **Nazis** but was sympathetic to Jews. Tivadar had the most trouble with his mother-in-law: "She couldn't see the dangers and refused to use a false identity." Tivadar at last persuaded her to live with a woman who had worked for the family.

Learning a New Identity

Tivadar's wife, Elizabeth, went to share the home of a friend of theirs. Her papers gave her a German background (harder to check than a Hungarian one) and made her a Catholic. Tivadar recalled:

> *I made up all kinds of difficult questions, which she learned to answer pretty well. We did not want her stumbling if the police questioned her. A Catholic friend taught her the **catechism.***

Tivadar set up a hiding place in a small, windowless room in the building he ran. A Jewish architect friend, Lajos, fixed the room with hidden ventilation, water, and electricity.

Moving Around

Tivadar was helping others to get **papers**. He realized he was in danger when people he hardly knew began coming to him for help. Too many people knew about his apartment. He moved to an apartment some friends were renting: "The rent was so high that you had to be a war-profiteer or a Jew in hiding to be willing to pay it." He moved from here to the hidden room: "I kept this address a secret, meeting people at a certain church at a set time each day."

Keeping in Touch

Although the Soros family had split up, they met when they could, in public places.

I met George at the public baths one morning and we exchanged news. The attendant recognized me, but did not know we were Jewish. I met George or Paul there from time to time.

Tivadar met Elizabeth in a local park and soon found that she was very unhappy where she was and worried that she was being watched. She said:

There was an air raid last night and I heard one of the boys down there whisper to another: "That's her!" Mrs. Zarvics [the woman she was staying with] *wants me to move to the country.*

Tivadar said she should go.

A Close Call

A few days after Elizabeth Soros moved to the country, the Budapest police came to question her, saying she was accused of being a Jewish **communist** who typed and sent out communist pamphlets. She proved she had no typewriter, which threw doubt on the whole accusation, so the police left. Elizabeth feared they would be back, and she could not cope with more questions. She fled back to Budapest and Tivadar. They decided she should move to another village. When Elizabeth settled down, George went to live in the same village, pretending to be her godson: "but I insisted they still lived separately, for safety.

Eyes Everywhere

Paul had been pretending to be a student, but his papers showed he was old enough to join the army. His landlady did not suspect he was Jewish, but kept asking why he had not joined the army yet. Tivadar found a way to change Paul's papers, making him seventeen again. This forced him to move, because his landlady had seen his old papers. Meanwhile, George came back to Budapest, to live with a Catholic family. Tivadar had to move again, too. The Nazis were moving the remaining Jews in Budapest into "Jewish houses"—Tivadar's hiding place was in one of these.

The Allies Invade Europe

The Allies invaded Europe in June 1944. These American troops are fighting at St. Malo, on the French coast. As troops advanced from both east and west, Tivadar hoped that the Nazis would begin to treat Jews better. Instead, things got worse and Nazi **propaganda** began having an effect:

> *Crimes against Jews went unpunished. There were cases of people promising to smuggle Jews out of the country then killing them along the way and taking their possessions.*

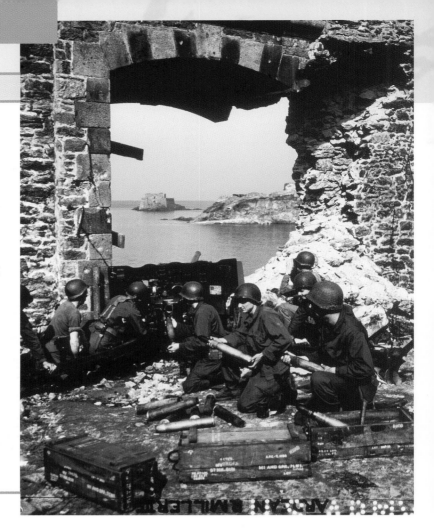

Too Confident?

By the end of the summer in 1944, the **Allies** seemed to be winning. Soviet troops were advancing from the east, while British and American troops were moving through occupied France. George, Paul, Tivadar, and his mother-in-law were all in Budapest. Elizabeth came back from the country, as did many others. Elizabeth suggested it was safe to come out of hiding. Tivadar wanted to wait. On October 15, Admiral Horthy, the Hungarian leader who had worked with the **Nazis,** said he had made peace with the Allies. Many submarines came out of hiding, but it was too soon. The Nazis simply took power by force and stepped up actions against **Jewish** people.

The Budapest Ghetto

In November 1944, a **ghetto** was set up in Budapest for the remaining Jews. Among the people swept into it was Tivadar's mother-in-law. He smuggled her out, and found her a place to stay with a Christian family that he suspected of being Jewish. Elizabeth quickly went back to the country, while Paul, George, and Tivadar stayed in Budapest. Jewish people were rounded up into the ghetto, killed on the street, or deported. People in the Jewish houses were either deported or made to work in **labor camps**. All of this happened despite the fact that the Nazis were clearly losing the war.

Tivadar remembers:

Conditions in the ghetto got worse and worse. The Nazis would turn up and shoot everyone in a building. . . . More and more stories leaked out about the German mass extermination camps. Even businessmen who had bought their freedom from Hungarian Nazis were caught.

The Last Months

In December 1944, Elizabeth was cut off from the rest of the family because of the war. Until this point they had been able to send messages from time to time. The Allies were now bombing Budapest and it was dangerous to be out on the street.

It got harder for George, Paul, and Tivadar to stay in touch. So the boys came to live in Tivadar's apartment, pretending to be his godsons. On Christmas Day they opened an unlabeled tin to celebrate: "To our great surprise it contained pineapple, a treat even before the war. We decided to eat it slowly, spreading it over five days." Finally, on February 13, 1945, the Nazis were driven out of Budapest by Soviet troops. Elizabeth returned to the city and the family was reunited.

Post-war Reunions

This photo shows a reunion of Hungarian Jewish survivors of the **Holocaust** in Budapest in 1946.

Timeline

1914–18	
	World War I is fought. It is ended by the **Treaty of Versailles.**
1923	
November 8	Hitler and the **Nazis** try to take power in Germany by force, but fail. Hitler is sent to prison but is released after nine months.
1933	
January 30	The Nazi Party comes to power in Germany. Adolf Hitler is elected Chancellor.
February 27	Fire breaks out at the Reichstag, the German Parliament.
February 28	Hindenburg's decree "For the Protection of the People and the State"allows for the creation of **concentration camps.** The Nazis persuaded Hindenburg to pass the decree to fight what they called the "**Communist** threat" after the Reichstag fire.
March 17	The **SS** is set up, formed as Hitler's bodyguard.
March 21	Dachau, the first Nazi concentration camp, is set up. Many more follow.
April 26	The **Gestapo** (Nazi secret police force) is formed.
May 2	Trade unions are banned in Germany.
May 10	The first major burning of "**degenerate**" books takes place.
July 14	Political parties other than the Nazi Party are banned in Germany.
1934	
February 7	All students have to spend six months in the "labor service."
July 20	The SS is now in charge of their own affairs—they are no longer part of the army.
August 2	Hitler makes himself *Führer*, sole leader of Germany.
1935	
September 15	The Nuremberg Laws are passed against German **Jews.**
1936	
August	The Olympics are held in Berlin.
1938	
March 13	Germany takes over Austria, which had once been part of Germany. The Austrian people vote to become part of Germany again.
August 8	Mauthausen concentration camp is set up.
October 28	The first group of Jews are deported from Poland by the Polish government.
November 9	Synagogues are burned and shops and homes are looted in Nazi-led violence against Jewish people known as *Kristallnacht*.
1939	
August 28	Rationing is introduced. Almost all food and items like clothes and gas are rationed.
September 1	Germany invades Poland. Nazis begin to pass laws against Polish Jews. The Soviet Union invades Poland from the east on September 17.
September 3	Britain and France declare war on Germany.
September 28	Germany and the Soviet Union split Poland up between them.
November 30	The Soviet Union invades Finland.

1940

February 12	German Jews are removed from their homes and taken to **ghettos** in Poland.
April 9	Germany invades Denmark and Norway.
April 27	Heinrich Himmler told to build a camp at Auschwitz.
April 30	A large ghetto is set up in the Polish city of Lodz. All Jews from the city and the surrounding area are sent there. More ghettos are planned in other Polish cities for Polish Jews, and then for Jews from other lands controlled by Germany.
May 10	Germany invades Belgium, France, Luxembourg, and the Netherlands
November 15	The Warsaw ghetto is set up.

1941

April 6	Germany invades Yugoslavia and Greece.
June 22	Germany invades the Soviet Union; mass executions of Soviet Jews follow.
September 1	All German Jews over the age of six have to wear a yellow Star of David.
From September	Mass gassings at Auschwitz begin with Soviet prisoners-of-war and continue. They focus on Jews and become more regular from January 1942.
October 10	The Terezín ghetto is set up; German and Czech Jews are sent there.
October 16	Mass **deportation** of German Jews to Poland begins.
October 28	10,000 Jews selected and killed at the Kovno ghetto, in Poland.
December 7	Japan bombs the American fleet at Pearl Harbor, bringing the U.S. into the war.
December 8	The first gassing of Jews takes place at Chelmno.
December 11	Germany and Italy declare war on the United States.

1942

January 20	Wannsee Conference outlines the "Final Solution" to the "Jewish Problem."
March 26	The first major British bombing raid on German cities takes place.
May 30–31	Cologne is bombed.

1943

March 17	Bulgaria and Hungary, allies of Germany, refuse to deport Jews.
April 19	The Warsaw ghetto revolt begins.
June 11	Himmler orders all remaining ghettos to be emptied and their inhabitants killed.

1944

March 23	Deportation of Jews from Greece (occupied by the Germans) begins.
April 9	Two Jews escape from Auschwitz and send news of the camp to the **Allies.**
May 15	Mass deportation and gassing of Hungarian Jews begins.
From June	Death marches from camps in the East. Prisoners are marched westward, away from the camps in the east, in front of advancing Soviet troops.
June 6	Allied troops land in Normandy.

1945

January 27	Soviet troops reach Auschwitz.
April 11	American troops reach Buchenwald.
April 15	British troops reach Belsen.
April 29	American troops reach Dachau.
April 30	Hitler commits suicide in Berlin, as the city is occupied by Soviet troops.
May 5	American troops reach Mauthausen.
May 7	Germany surrenders.
November 20	Nuremberg trials of Nazi war criminals begin.

Glossary

Ally country that fought against Nazi Germany in World War II

anti-Semitism prejudiced against Jewish people; someone who does not like Jews is *anti-Semitic*

Aryan race invented by the Nazis to mean people with northern European ancestors, without any ancestors from so-called inferior races, such as Poles, Slavs, or Jews. Aryans were usually thought to be blonde, blue-eyed and sturdy.

asocial Nazi term for people who did not support the Nazi state. Asocials could be drunks, people who would not work, homosexuals, or members of a religious group whose beliefs might make them oppose the Nazis.

blitzkrieg German for "lightning war;" used to describe the German tactic of invading a country at high speed

catechism way of teaching the Christian religion—it is a list of question and answers that summarize the religion

citizen person who belongs to a country and who has rights in that country, such as protection by the law, and duties to that country, such as paying taxes

collaborate to work with another person or country; in war, to betray your country by doing this

Communist person who believes that a country should be governed by the people of that country for the good of everyone in it. They believe private property is wrong, including owning a home to running a business. The state should own everything and run everything, giving the people the things they need.

concentration camp prison camp set up by the Nazis under a special law that meant that the prisoners were never tried and were never given a release date. The Nazis could put anyone in these camps, for any reason or none, for as long as they wanted.

death camp camp set up by the Nazis to murder as many people, most of them Jewish, as quickly and cheaply as possible. Most of the victims were gassed.

degenerate someone who the Nazis saw as having very low moral standards

democracy system of government in which people vote for representatives; the people are free to choose who has power and how that power should be used

deportation being sent away from a place and not allowed to return

eugenics lesson in Nazi schools that taught girls about the characteristics to look for in a perfect husband and father

Gestapo secret police set up by the Nazis in 1933

ghetto area of a town or city, walled or fenced off from the rest of the city, where Jewish people were forced to live

Gypsy member of a traveling people who speak the Romany language; the Nazis used the word "Gypsy" to describe all traveling or homeless people, or even those whose ancestors had been travelers or homeless

Hitler Youth Nazi organization for boys that trained them to be fit and obedient to the Nazis. Boys were trained to become good soldiers. Girls had to join a girls' movement that trained them to be good wives and mothers.

Holocaust huge destruction or sacrifice. When it appears with a capital "H," it refers to the deliberate attempt by the Nazi government in Germany to destroy all of the Jewish people in their power.

Jehovah's Witnesses religious group that was especially persecuted by the Nazis because members refused to swear an oath of loyalty to Hitler

Jew (Jewish) someone who follows the Jewish faith. The Nazis also called people Jews if they had Jewish ancestors, even if they had changed their faith.

Judenfrei "Jew free;" a place with no Jewish people living there

kindergarten nursery school that children go to until they are six years old

labor camps camp set up by the Nazis that was a prison that used the prisoners as cheap labor

Lebensraum German word for "living-space." Hitler was trying to provide more land for Germans to live on.

Nazi member of the Nazi Party. Nazi is short for *Nationalsozialistische Deutsche Arbeiterpartei*, the National Socialist German Workers' Party.

occupied used in this book to mean a country that has been captured by Germany and is ruled by Nazis supported by the German army

papers used in this book to mean all the different documents needed under Nazi rule: identity card, work permit, travel permit, Aryan certificate, and so on

political having to do with ideas and actions of government; person arrested for opposing Nazi ideas or actions

propaganda information and ideas that are worded and presented so that people will accept and believe them even if they are not true

protective custody arrest under the law, "For the Protection of the People and the State," passed in February 1933, that allowed the German police to arrest people for as long as they like without bringing them to trial

race group of people with the same ancestors

racial inferiority/superiority Nazis believed that some races were inferior, that is, not as good as other races. They believed the Jewish people belonged to a separate race, one that was inferior to the German Aryan race (which the Nazis invented). According to the Nazis, the German Aryans were a superior race.

Reich empire. *See* Third Reich.

Reichmark (RM) German money under the Nazis

SA (short for *Sturmabteilung*) storm troopers. This was Hitler and the Nazis' first private army. Their violence helped the Nazis to win the 1932 election.

SS (short for *Schutzstaffel*) security staff. The SS began as Hitler's personal bodyguard. Later, they ran concentration camps and death camps. Everyone in the SS swore loyalty to Hitler, rather than Germany.

Sudetenland part of Czechoslovakia that had once been part of Germany

swastika equal armed cross with each arm bent at a right angle in a clockwise direction. It was the symbol adopted by the Nazi party.

Third Reich "the third empire." The Nazis saw their rule as the third German empire, with Hitler as the emperor, or *Führer*.

transit camp camp where people were imprisoned temporarily before being sent somewhere else

Treaty of Versailles treaty that ended World War I. It took a lot of land and military power away from Germany.

undesirable word used by the Nazis to describe any person that they did not approve of because of political beliefs, race, religion, or behavior.

World War I war fought in Europe between 1914 and 1918

Further Reading

Frank, Anne. *Diary of a Young Girl.* Columbus, Ohio: Prentice Hall, 1993.

Shuter, Jane. *Auschwitz.* Chicago: Heinemann Library, 1999.

Tames, Richard. *Anne Frank.* Chicago: Heinemann Library, 1998.

Tames, Richard. *Adolf Hitler.* Chicago: Heinemann Library, 1998.

Whittock, Martyn. *Hitler & National Socialism.* Chicago: Heinemann Library, 1996.

Wiesel, Elie. *Night.* New York: Bantam Books, 1982.

Willoughby, Susan. *The Holocaust.* Chicago: Heinemann Library, 2000.

Sources

The author and publishers gratefully acknowledge the publications from which written sources in the book are drawn. In somes cases the wording or sentence structure has been simplified to make the material suitable for a school readership.

Bielenberg, Christabel. *The Past is Myself.* Minneapolis: Irish Books & Media, Incorporated, 1982. (p. 22)

Dobrosszycki, Lucjan (editor). *Chronicle of the Lodz Ghetto 1941–44.* New Haven, Conn.: Yale University Press, 1984. (pp. 37, 39)

Dwork, Deborah and Robert Jan van Pelt. *Auschwitz: 1270 to Present.* Scranton, Penn.: W. W. Norton & Company, 1996. (pp. 7, 34)

Fox, Anne. *My Heart in a Suitcase.* Portland, Oreg.: Vallentine Mitchell Publishers, 1996. (p. 22)

Gibbon, Constantine Fritz and Krystyna Michalik (translators). *KL Auschwitz Seen by the SS.* Oswiecim, Poland: Auschwitz Birkenau State Museum, 1998. (p. 41)

Gilbert, Martin. *The Boys: The Story of 732 Young Concentration Camp Survivors.* New York: Heny Holt & Company, 1997. (pp. 38, 39)

Gilbert, Martin. *Never Again: A History of the Holocaust.* New York: Universe Publishing, 2000. (p. 30)

Gut Opdyke, Irene. *In My Hands: Memories of a Holocaust Rescuer.* Westminster, Md.: Alfred A. Knopf Books for Young Readers, 1999. (pp. 12, 27)

Hahn, Edith. *The Nazi Officer's Wife.* Brookline Village, Mass.: Abacus Press, 1999. (p. 44)

Harris, Mark Jonathan and Deborah Oppenheimer. *Into the Arms of Strangers.* New York: Bloomsbury Publishing, 2000. (p. 17)

Noakes, J. and G. Pridham. *Nazism, 1919–1945.* Exeter, UK: University of Exeter Press, 1991. (pp. 11, 16, 18)

Rees, Laurence. *The Nazis: A Warning from History.* New York: The New Press, 1999. (pp. 19, 24, 26, 40)

Soros, Tivadar, Paul Soros, and George Soros. *Maskerado: Dancing Around Death in Nazi Hungary.* Edinburgh, UK: Canongate Books, 2001. © Tivadar Soros, 1965. (pp. 45–49)

Townsend, Colin & Eileen. *War Wives.* New York: Grafton Publications, Incorporated, 1989. (pp. 24, 25)

Ungerer, Tomi. *Tomi: A Childhood Under the Nazis.* Lanhan, Md.: Roberts Rinehart, 1998. (p. 13)

Places of Interest and Websites

Florida Holocaust Museum
55 Fifth Street South
St. Petersburg, FL 33701
Visitor information: (727) 820-0100
Website: *http://www.flholocaustmuseum.org*

Holocaust Memorial Center
6602 West Maple Road
West Bloomfield, MI 48322
Visitor information: (248) 661-0840
Website: *http://holocaustcenter.org*

Holocaust Museum Houston
5401 Caroline Street
Houston, TX 77004
Visitor information: (713) 942-8000
Website: *http://www.hmh.org*

Simon Wiesenthal Center: Museum of Tolerance
Simon Wiesenthal Plaza
9786 West Pico Blvd.
Los Angeles, CA 90035
Visitor information: (310) 553-8403
Website: *http://www.museumoftolerance.com*

United States Holocaust Memorial Museum
100 Raoul Wallenberg Place, SW
Washington, D.C. 20024
Visitor information: (202) 488-0400
Website: *http://www.ushmm.org*

Website warning
1. Almost all Holocaust websites have been designed for adult users. They may contain horrifying and upsetting information and pictures.
2. Some people wish to minimize the Holocaust, or even deny that it happened at all. Some of their websites pretend to be delivering unbiased facts and information. To be sure of getting accurate information, it is always best to use an officially recognized site such as the ones listed on this page.
3. If you plan to visit a Holocaust website, ask an adult to view the site with you.

Disclaimer
All the Internet addresses (URLs) given in this book were valid at the time of going to press. However, due to the dynamic nature of the Internet, some addresses may have changed, or sites may have ceased to exist since publication. While the author and publisher regret any inconvenience this may cause readers, no responsibility for any such changes can be accepted by either the author or the publisher.

Index